JAGUARS

Sandie Lee Books

Jaguars

Jaguars are the third largest cat in the world. They are powerful wild cats, but are not known to attack humans. Jaguars were once highly esteemed in the ancient Native American cultures. They were used and portrayed as royal symbols. People in this time thought the jaguar could protect them from evil. The name "jaguar" is a native American word (yaguar) which means "he who kills with one leap." Check out some more cool facts about this big cat.

Where in the World?

Did you know the jaguar was once found around the US/Mexico border? Due to poaching, the jaguar's numbers have fallen. The largest population of jaguars live in remote areas in South and Central America, mostly in the Amazon Basin. They like all habitats from swampy lowlands to grassy and forested regions.

The Body of a Jaguar

Did you know the jaguar is very powerful? It has a stout body, with a wide head and roundish ears. It can measure up to 6 feet long from the tip of its tail to its nose. The jaguar can also weigh up to 220 pounds. Females will be smaller than the males.

The Coat of a Jaguar

Did you know the jaguar has a remarkable coat? Its beautiful coat can be yellow, tan, reddish-brown or black with bold black spots. These spots are solid on its head and neck. They become larger and more ring-like along the side and back of the body. They are called "rosettes."

What a Jaguar Eats

Did you know jaguars eat only meat? This large cat is a carnivore or meat-eater. It will eat most anything it can catch like snakes, deer, monkeys, sloths, turtles, various eggs, frogs and fish. The jaguar can eat up to 55 pounds of meat in one feeding. It gorges itself on its kill to keep full until its next hunt.

The Jaguar's Special Ability

Did you know this wild cat likes water? In fact, the jaguar prefers to live next to rivers and swamps. It is a powerful swimmer and will bathe, play and lounge in a body of water. It is also a fast runner, reaching top speeds of up to 40 miles-per-hour for short sprints.

The Jaguar as a Predator

Did you know this animal is a great hunter? The jaguar is called an ambush predator. This means it will sneak up on its prey, rather than chase it down. This cat will lunge with great force onto its prey and bite it around the neck or head. Once the animal is dead, the jaguar will drag it away to eat it.

The Jaguar as Prey

Did you know jaguars will hunt each other? Jaguars are very protective of their territory and will fight and even kill another jaguar. Man is also a predator to the jaguar. Because of this large cat's pelt, man has poached them for their fur. It is now illegal to hunt a jaguar.

The Powerful Jaguar

Did you know the jaguar is very strong? This large cat has so much force in its jaw alone, it can crush the skull of its large prey. The jaguar uses it strong legs, neck and jaws to carry its prey away to eat it. Sometimes this is up a tree or across a large body of water.

Jaguar Talk

Did you know jaguars can communicate? Like most large wild cats, the jaguar can roar. But when it roars it comes out sounding like a deep chesty cough. It may do this to defend its territory. Other sounds include grunting and mewing. Just like a pet cat, jaguars can also purr.

The Jaguar Mom

Did you know the mother jaguar is fiercely protective of her young? A female jaguar can become pregnant when she is only 3 years-old. She will carry her young from 90 to 110 days. Before she is ready to give birth, she will find a safe and sheltered den or thicket to have her babies in.

The Jaguar Baby

Did you know baby jaguars are called kittens? There can be anywhere from 1 to 4 kittens born at one time. They weigh about 4 pounds each and have fuzzy spotted coats. They nurse milk from their mother. When they are 6 months old they will begin to hunt on their own.

Jaguars at Rest

Did you know jaguars spend 45 percent of their time sleeping and resting? Jaguars will sleep around 10 hours each day. They do this high up in a tree or under one. They will also take a snooze in the tall grass. This cat likes to feel safe, so it will always sleep in a well hidden spot.

Life of a Jaguar

Did you know jaguars have a huge home range? Male jaguars call between 19 to 53 square miles their own. The female's territory is smaller and is between 10 to 37 square miles. In nature, jaguars can live to be up to 15 years-old. In captivity they can reach ages of around 18 to 20 years-old.

Black Jaguars

Jaguars can have a dark coat that looks almost like it is solid black. However, if you were to look closely, you would see it still has spots. The black jaguar is usually found in the darker regions of the rainforest. They are somewhat rare, but are just as powerful as the other jaguars.

Quiz

Question 1: The native word for jaguar is, "yaguar." What does this mean?

Answer 1: He who kills with one leap

Question 2: How big does a male jaguar grow to?

Answer 2: It can be 6 feet long and 220 pounds

Question 3: The jaguar is an *ambush hunter*. What does this mean?

Answer 3: The jaguar will sneak up on its prey rather than chase it down

Question 4: What is special about the jaguar's jaws?

Answer 4: They are so strong they can crush the skull of a large animal

Question 5: What is another type of jaguar?

Answer 5: The black jaguar. Its coat is very dark in color.

Thank you for checking out another addition from Sandie Lee Books! Make sure to check out Amazon.com for many other great titles.

www.ingramcontent.com/pod-product-compliance
Lightning Source LLC
Chambersburg PA
CBHW050801290526
45792CB00008B/2284